C000179199

BRITISH RAILWAYS

PAST and PRESENT

No 51

ISLE OF WIGHT CENTRAL RAILWAYS.

_____ STATION,

No. 11725   Date_____ 18__

EXCESS FARE RECEIPT.

To what Station.	Particulars of Excess.	Amount. £ s. d

Number of Annual or
Season Ticket   _____ Signature_____

N.B.-This Note to be shown when required by the Company's Servants, and given up at the end of the Journey; and if issued to a Season Ticket Holder, the Season Ticket must be produced when the note is given up.

When this receipt is issued to a Season Ticket Holder, it is only available for the same period an ordinary Ticket would be between the places named on this Excess Note; also when issued for a double journey, it is only available for the first journey on the date of issue.

Issued subject to the Company's published rules and regulations.

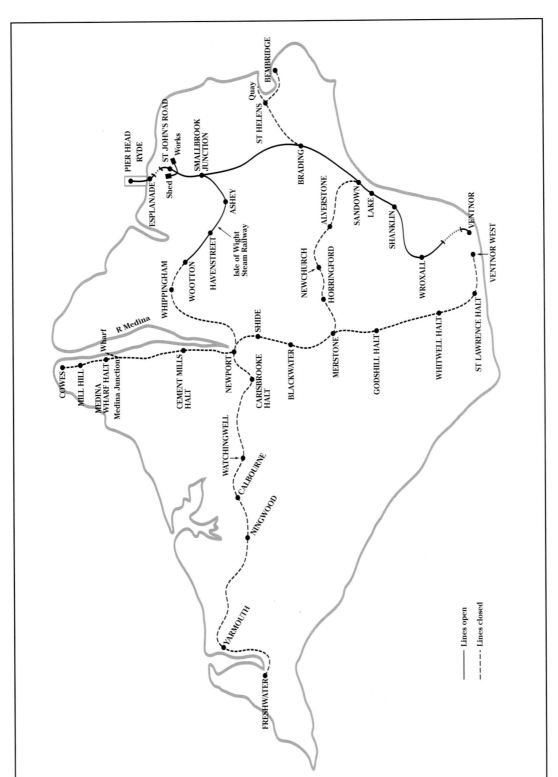

Map of the railways of the Isle of Wight, showing locations featured or referred to in the text.

BRITISH RAILWAYS

PAST and PRESENT

No 51

Isle of Wight

Terry Gough ARPS

Past and Present

Past & Present Publishing Ltd

© Terry Gough 2005

All rights reserved. No part of this publication may be reproduced, stored in a retrieval system or transmitted, in any form or by any means, electronic, mechanical, photocopying, recording or otherwise, without prior permission in writing from Past & Present Publishing Ltd.

First published in 2005
Reprinted 2007

British Library Cataloguing in Publication Data

A catalogue record for this book is available from the British Library.

ISBN 978 1 85895 179 9

Past & Present Publishing Ltd
The Trundle
Ringstead Road
Great Addington
Kettering
Northants NN14 4BW

Tel/Fax: 01536 330588
email: sales@nostalgiacollection.com
Website: www.nostalgiacollection.com

Printed and bound in the Czech Republic

All photographs were taken by the author unless otherwise credited and all items of ephemera are from the author's collection.

Title page **Isle of Wight Central Railway excess fare ticket issued at Horringford on 6 August 1890.**

SANDOWN: Up and down trains cross during the last week of steam operation in the winter of 1966. By this time most of the locomotives were in a poor condition, despite the best efforts of both Works and Shed staff.

On the evening of 4 May 2004 Class 483 No 006 in 'dinosaur' livery enters Sandown on its way south. There are two trains per hour (unevenly spaced), and alternate trains pass here.

CONTENTS

RYDE ST JOHN'S ROAD: Descending the bank from Smallbrook Junction to Ryde St John's Road on 4 August 1959 is Class 'O2' No 28 *Ashey* with Set No 490 on the 5.08pm from Newport to Ryde Pier Head.

Twenty-eight years later a former London Underground train, now Class 485 No 485045, heads away from Ryde on an afternoon train to Shanklin.

INTRODUCTION

Much has been published about the railways of the Isle of Wight in steam days, for the very good reason that the system was akin to a living museum of pre-Grouping locomotives and rolling-stock, all of which were well maintained and smartly presented. The network was extensive, the main routes being from Ryde to Ventnor and Ryde to Cowes via Newport. There were branches to Bembridge, Freshwater and Ventnor West, and a line connecting Newport with Sandown.

The short section from Ryde Pier Head to St John's Road was jointly owned by the London, Brighton & South Coast Railway (LBSCR) and London & South Western Railway (LSWR), over which the Island companies exercised running powers. There were three of the latter, the largest of which was the Isle of Wight Central Railway (IWCR). This company owned lines from Newport to Cowes, Ventnor Town (later named Ventnor West), Sandown and Ryde St John's Road. It also operated the Freshwater, Yarmouth & Newport Railway (FYNR) until 1913. The Isle of Wight Railway (IWR) ran from St John's Road to Ventnor, with a branch from Brading to Bembridge. The IWCR and IWR were absorbed into the Southern Railway (SR) at the beginning of 1923 and the FYNR followed in August of the same year.

The SR inherited an antiquated and miscellaneous collection of motive power and rolling-stock. This included four ex-LBSCR 'A1s' and 'A1Xs' (known as 'Terriers') owned by the IWCR and one by the FYNR. The SR embarked on a modernisation programme by transferring stock from the mainland. Locomotives were predominantly ex-LSWR Class 'O2' 0-4-4 tank engines; the first two arrived on the Island in 1923 and the last two in 1949. Four LBSCR 'E1' 0-6-0s were transferred in 1932/33. There was also movement of 'Terriers': one was withdrawn in 1926, then the SR imported a further three between 1927 and 1930. However, increased train weights followed by track improvements resulted in four being returned to the mainland in 1936. Of the remaining three, one went back to the mainland in 1947, followed by the final two in 1949. More recently the Isle of Wight Steam Railway (IWSR) has acquired two (IWCR No 11 and FYNR No 2). Other classes were considered by the SR for use on the Island, but found unsuitable. Locomotive numbers were prefixed by 'W' by the SR, although this was omitted from the cabside from 1931.

During its first eight years the SR, after importing nine LSWR bogie coaches, gradually replaced the Island companies' coaching stock with four-wheeled vehicles of LBSCR and London, Chatham & Dover Railway (LCDR) origin. It then transferred LCDR and LBSCR bogie stock to replace the four-wheelers, but after the Second World War it withdrew the LCDR bogies in favour of SECR vehicles. Many transferred coaches were modified for use on the Island. The SR formed coaches into sets, but, unlike on the mainland, they were not permanent, being altered to suit the level of traffic and availability of coaches, particularly in the final years of operation. The SR also imported replacement goods vehicles, which were mostly of LBSCR and LSWR origin. Much later a few SR four-wheeled utility vans and some open wagons were sent to the Island.

The SR rationalised train services, with the most heavily used section from Ryde to Ventnor seeing an intensive service, which continued right up to the end of steam. Below is an attempt at summarising the services, although there were exceptions to the patterns described.

Immediately prior to the Second World War the Freshwater line had a train approximately every 1½ hours each way on weekdays. All trains called at all stations other than Watchingwell, which was by request and was not in the public timetable. Services were less frequent on Sundays. In the 1950s there were also two through trains, one from Ventnor and the other from Sandown; the former was fast from Sandown to Newport, then Yarmouth and Freshwater. There was still no reference to Watchingwell.

Over the same period services from Cowes to Ventnor West ran about every other hour, but none on Sundays. Trains ran between Newport and Sandown mostly every other hour, with fewer trains on Sundays.

Pre-war services between Ryde and Cowes were about half-hourly on weekdays and less frequent on Sundays. Post-war the service was hourly every day of the week during the summer, but bi-hourly on winter Sundays.

Ryde to Ventnor was approximately half-hourly on weekdays and hourly on Sundays during the summer. In the winter it was hourly every day. Brading to Bembridge trains ran every half an hour, including part of Sundays.

The first line to close was Merstone to Ventnor West in 1952, followed a year later by Newport to Freshwater and Brading to Bembridge. Then at the beginning of 1956 Newport to Sandown closed. Only the two main routes (Ryde to Ventnor and Ryde to Newport and Cowes) remained open, and these were still intensively worked during summer weekends, with trains often crowded to capacity. Several excuses were made for effecting complete closure of the system, and it was clear that, whatever the future, the ancient stock could not be economically maintained any longer. In the event, the line to Newport and Cowes was closed completely in February 1966 and the Shanklin to Ventnor section two months later. The Ryde to Shanklin section was retained and electrified during early 1967. It seemed rather short-sighted to isolate Ventnor, a popular holiday resort, and although a dedicated bus connection with the train at Shanklin was provided, this was short-lived, and it was not until October 2004 that a proper rail/bus connection with selected trains at Shanklin was re-instated. It also seemed undesirable to isolate Newport, the Island's capital, from the railway system in view of the poor road access. There were plans for a private company to run a railcar service on the Newport line, but the scheme collapsed in 1970.

The unique solution to the stock replacement problem was found in using withdrawn London Transport Underground coaches. All services were suspended between January and March 1967 while the line from Ryde to Shanklin was electrified using the third-rail SR system. After overhaul and modification, the Underground coaches were transferred to the Island and services resumed on 20 March 1967. Stock consisted of 1923 trailer coaches and 1931-34 motor coaches, mostly from the Northern and Piccadilly Lines. They were delivered by road from Fratton to Ryde St John's Road via the Portsmouth to Fishbourne car ferry; formed into six four-car sets (numbered 041-046) and six three-car sets (031-036), they were given the SR-style classifications 4-VEC and 3-TIS respectively, obviously derived from Vectis, the Latin name for the Island. This at least made it clear that they belonged on the Island, unlike their subsequent classifications of 485 and 486. The new railway was referred to as 'Ryde Rail', which was displayed on the trains. At the time of the conversion, it was anticipated that this would only be a stopgap measure and that within a few years the Island would have no railway at all. Although some of the coaches were withdrawn, even 20 years later there were still seven sets in running order, by then reformed into two- and five-car units.

In keeping with the Island's tradition of using other people's leftovers, it was decided to replace the first Underground trains with more modern stock from the same source. In 1989/90 eight two-car units from 1938 Northern Line Underground stock were converted for use on the Island. A further unit was converted in 1992 and two spare bodyshells were also transferred for possible use in the event of damage to existing units. All these vehicles had been withdrawn by London Underground in 1985, but refurbished a year later to cover stock shortages, when they had been repainted in old Underground red livery. On the Island they are referred to as Class 483, and six units are still in operation today, on what is now called 'Island Line', a Stagecoach Group company. This was yet another short-term solution, and various options for the future are under consideration, including conversion to a tramway or, as always, closure. When transferred they carried Network South East livery, now replaced by a special Island Line livery incorporating dinosaurs – it seems an unusual marketing strategy to promote services with an implication of extinction. Two units have recently been repainted in original London Underground livery.

When the electric trains were introduced, there was an hourly service in the winter and half-hourly on summer weekdays, with additional trains running only to Sandown. Trains were even more frequent on summer Saturdays. The weekday service was later increased to three trains per hour equally spaced and crossing at Ryde St John's Road, and between Brading and Sandown. This was later reduced to two per hour and hourly on Sundays, but by summer 1987 there were again three trains per hour. In the early 1990s the timetable was changed to give two trains per hour at unequal intervals. This is the current position, with trains passing alternately between Ryde St John's Road and Smallbrook Junction, and at Sandown.

Despite shrinkage and rationalisation of the railway, there have also been some new developments. In 1987 a new station was opened at Lake, between Sandown and Shanklin. Steam trains can still be seen on the Island, despite apparent elimination in 1966, at Havenstreet, between Ryde and Newport, the headquarters of the Isle of Wight Steam Railway. A solitary Class 'O2', No 24 *Calbourne*, and some coaches and wagons were saved from scrap and stored at Newport until the beginning of 1971, when the engine hauled the stock to Havenstreet. This was the last ever train to leave Newport, as shortly afterwards dismantling of the railway began. Havenstreet station was re-opened to the public in the spring of the same year and limited services were run between Havenstreet and Wootton. It was not until 1986 that Wootton had a station again and passengers could alight. In 1991 the Steam Railway extended its track eastward to an interchange with the electric railway on the site of Smallbrook Junction, where a new station was built. The intermediate station of Ashey was re-opened as a request stop in 1993. Track for this section of the line was obtained from Ryde Rail when it singled its line between Sandown and Brading in 1989. There had never been a station at Smallbrook, and the new station is solely for interchange purposes with the Island Line trains to Ryde and Shanklin.

The author's first visit to the Island's railways was on a day trip in June 1953. He returned for a longer stay at the end of 1955. There was no room at the local inn, so he made his base in a coach stabled in the sidings at Sandown. He was awakened early after the first night to find his freezing-cold 'bedroom' on the move, as it was to form the first train of the day to Newport. He stayed on the train as far as Alverstone, then, to warm up, walked (with authority) along the track to Newchurch to await the arrival of the second train. Permission is no longer required because the trackbed is now a public cycle path. Subsequent visits during the steam era were made annually until closure of the last line to Newport. He made visits following introduction of the Underground trains and to see the Isle of Wight Steam Railway, then made several visits more recently to gather the present-day material for this book. All visits, other than one in 2004, have been exclusively by public transport and by walking.

Terry Gough
Sherborne

ACKNOWLEDGEMENTS

The closed stations, where they still exist, are on private property and the various owners are thanked for permission to enter their land. British Railways is thanked for the provision of a lineside pass. Roger Silsbury is thanked for providing several photographs from the archives of the Isle of Wight Steam Railway and for the provision of information. Richard Casserley, Lawrence Golden and Barry Thirlwall have, as always, been most helpful in providing photographs from their own collections. My wife, Cynthia, is thanked for her contribution, which started by posing outside Ventnor station in 1957.

BIBLIOGRAPHY

Bradley, D. L. *A Locomotive History of the Railways of the Isle of Wight* (RCTS 1982; ISBN 0 901115 57 6)

Gough, Terry *The Southern Railway Collection: Branch Lines Recalled* (Silver Link Publishing, 1991; ISBN 1 85794 126 8)

Pomeroy, Colin *Isle of Wight Railways* (Silver Link Publishing, 1991; ISBN 1 947971 62 9)

AUTHOR'S NOTES

Much has changed on the Island since publication in 1991 of Colin Pomeroy's excellent book on the 'then and now' theme; these changes can be seen in the photographs, and comments are made in the associated captions. Wherever possible I have shown the locations from a different perspective. However, in a few instances nothing has changed and this is sometimes compounded by no alternative viewpoint being available. In such cases the photographs in the two books are remarkably similar, but this in itself is instructive.

Unless otherwise stated, the locomotives depicted are the ubiquitous Class 'O2' tanks.

Newport

NEWPORT: In a spirited departure from Newport on 12 August 1965, Class O2 No 16 *Ventnor* heads for Cowes. The Freshwater line, long closed, curves to the right; an SR utility van is in the former Freshwater line bay platform. The line from Ryde passes by the terrace of houses in the distance.

The elimination of the station and surrounding area has been complete. It is very difficult to find the exact location because of the lack of surviving landmarks and the changes in level of the ground, but there are just a few clues that confirm that this is the present-day (5 May 2004) equivalent view.

NEWPORT: A closer view of the station from the other side of the track shows another train heading for Cowes on 4 August 1959. This is the 3.30pm from Ryde Pier Head, hauled by another Class 'O2', this time No 17 *Seaview*.

The town lies to the right, and it is the church tower that enables the present view to be located.

NEWPORT: A short distance north of the station, in the summer of 1966, are large stockpiles of coal in ancient wooden-bodied wagons, mostly from the pre-Grouping era. The signal gantry guards the entrance to the station against trains from Cowes and Medina Wharf.

Changes in levels following demolition of the railway make an exact comparison impossible. The main road, seen on the previous pages, is to the right on the embankment. It is at about this point that the main road deviates from the course of the railway.

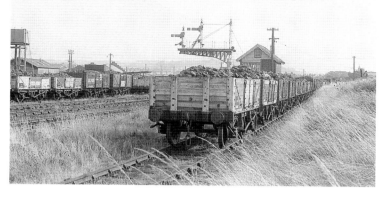

Below On 4 August 1959 the 4.24pm from Cowes to Ryde Pier Head approaches Newport behind engine No 17 *Seaview*. The driver has just handed the single-line token to the signalman.

NEWPORT: A short distance beyond the signal box, a welcome change from passenger trains on 20 September 1965 is the arrival of a coal train from Medina Wharf, headed by No 21 *Sandown*. There are two brake-vans on the train and two more in the siding to the right, all of which are ex-LSWR; indeed, there were no SR brake-vans on the Island.

Today's equivalent view is through an industrial estate. The main road lies to the left out of sight. The hill and woods in the background confirm the alignment.

NEWPORT: Trains cross at the south end of the station on 20 September 1965. The approaching train, from Ryde, is hauled by No 17 *Seaview*, which always seemed to feature frequently on the author's visits. The train from Cowes is headed by No 31 *Chale*. The viaduct in the background carries the line over the River Medina.

In 2004 the author found that the viaduct had been replaced by a new bridge carrying the main road. Alignment is again confirmed by some of the houses in the background and, of course, by the river.

NEWPORT: The remnant of the Freshwater branch was used for breaking up rolling-stock when the lines closed, and many historic vehicles were destroyed here in the winter of 1966/67. In the background are two pre-Grouping brake-vans, awaiting the same fate. They were sometimes referred to as 'road vans' as they were also used for carrying parcels.

A new local road has been built on the site and there are few clues to the existence of a railway. The alignment was deduced from buildings behind the camera.

NEWPORT: Beautiful wooden-bodied coaches from the SECR and LBSCR were also destroyed, and were stored a little closer to the junction with the Cowes-Newport line. The right foreground is the site of the short-lived station built by the FYNR while it was denied access to the IWCR station immediately before the First Word War. In the background is the former engine repair shed.

Today there is no obvious trace of the railway, and a minor road has been built through the 'graveyard' . The bridge carries the main road shown on earlier pages.

Newport to Cowes

MILL POND VIADUCT: From the outskirts of Newport the line to Cowes ran north alongside the River Medina. The first point of interest is Mill Pond Viaduct, which takes the railway over Dodnor Creek and a tributary of the Medina. On 14 August 1965 No 16 *Ventnor* takes a train from Cowes to Ryde over the viaduct.

Dodnor Creek, visited on 9 April 2004, is now a nature reserve and the trackbed is part of the National Cycle Route.

CEMENT MILLS HALT: A short distance further north was a cement works, which had its own halt and sidings. The halt did not appear in the public timetable, as its primary purpose was to serve the works. However, the main road between Newport and Cowes was within walking distance and passed through a residential area at this point. A train to Cowes stops briefly at the halt on 16 August 1965.

This is the same location on 9 April 2004. The remains of the halt can be found in the undergrowth immediately beyond the gates.

MEDINA JUNCTION is seen here on 16 August 1965, the line curving to the right descending to the Wharf. Until the early 1960s the Wharf was very busy and there were daily freight trains (mostly conveying coal) to other parts of the Island. There was also an unadvertised halt here, out of sight beyond the train on the right-hand side. Today the site of the junction is marked by the gap in the hedge on the right.

MEDINA JUNCTION: Engine No 22 *Brading* is seen near Medina Junction on a train bound for Cowes in 1965.
The present-day view looking toward Newport is much more restricted, with overhanging trees on both sides
of the trackbed. The cycle path is well used and is a shorter and safer way to travel between the two towns.

MEDINA WHARF still gives the appearance of being busy, even in the autumn of 1965. In reality some of the wagons are being used to store rather than transfer coal elsewhere.

Much of the Wharf is now in use by various industrial concerns, although the southern edge, where the 'past' photograph was taken, awaits development. Part is in use as a landfill site and the view therefore looks rather different from 40 years earlier.

MILL HILL station, on the edge of Cowes, was in a cramped location in a residential area. At the northern end, beyond the rear of the train, was a tunnel giving access to Cowes itself. Note the advertisement for excursions to Paris, predating Eurostar by three decades.

The station site has been cleared and is now a public park, known as Artic Gardens.

COWES: This 'aerial' view of the station was a favourite of photographers and gave by far the best vantage point. An unidentified Class 'O2' is running round its train, prior to returning to Ryde on 12 August 1965.

The view has changed dramatically since the railway closed. Virtually nothing remains to link the past, other than the vantage point itself. Until recently it was still possible to look down on the site of the station, but in April 2004 newly constructed flats have blocked the traditional view for ever.

COWES: On 20 September 1965 No 26 *Whitwell* backs out of the station to collect its coaches. Cowes was a neat little terminus, conveniently situated for the town, but some distance from the ferry terminal, thus limiting its potential.

All this has been swept away and in its place is a small supermarket and Admiral Gardens. This is the view looking toward the site of the buffer stops in April 2004.

Newport to Freshwater

CARISBROOKE HALT: The author first visited Carisbrooke on 29 December 1955, having arrived on the Island two days previously. The station had closed with the whole line on 21 September 1953, but still gave the impression that the last train had only just left. The station signs are still in place and there is no evidence of vandalism.

Since that time Newport has expanded westward and has subsumed Carisbrooke. The station site is now occupied by a school and playing fields, and the surrounding area is mainly residential. The railway ran close to the fence on the left.

WATCHINGWELL: The line climbed virtually all the way from Newport to within about a mile of Watchingwell, the ruling gradient being 1 in 63. Watchingwell was an isolated station with a very short platform, and there was no metalled road access; it was built as a private station and rarely featured in public timetables. It is shown as closed on the 1947 edition of the Ordnance Survey map, but in fact closed on the same day as the other stations on the line. This close-up photograph, showing the station in use, was taken on 3 September 1952.

The building still stands and is in use as a private dwelling. Privacy is maintained by trees and hedges, so that even in winter only a small part of the former station is visible from the adjacent public footpath – an enviable situation. The site of the boarded crossing is in the middle distance where the high hedge ends. *H. C. Casserley/TG*

CALBOURNE, although on a minor road, was much more accessible. On 3 September 1952 a train from Freshwater to Newport is just leaving and the signalman is preparing to open the gates to the road. The station was referred to as Calbourne & Shalfleet in the public timetable for many years, but the platform nameboards only displayed 'Calbourne'.

There is little trace of the railway today, and the site is occupied by a bungalow. The line ran past the side of the bungalow towards the photographer, who is standing in the road just forward of the signalman in the 'past' photograph. *H. C. Casserley/TG*

NINGWOOD: Just over a mile west of Calbourne the railway passed under another minor road and here was situated Ningwood station, serving the nearby hamlet. This general view of the station is looking toward Freshwater shortly before closure. The road bridge is behind the camera.

Road realignment has completely changed the view. The road overbridge has been removed, but the present photograph was taken from where the bridge once stood. The station was situated beyond the trees that are in the foreground. *IWSR Archive/TG*

YARMOUTH station was situated in a residential area on the edge of town, about 10 minutes' walk from the ferry terminal. Under the station nameboard is a sign that advises passengers to 'Alight here for slipway for boats to Lymington'. This photograph was taken about 1950.

The station building still stands and an additional building, not quite in the same attractive style, has been erected on the platform. The buildings are in use as a youth and community centre, seen here in spring 2004, while the trackbed is a cycle and bridle path to Freshwater. In the opposite direction the path only uses the trackbed for about half a mile. *IWSR Archive/TG*

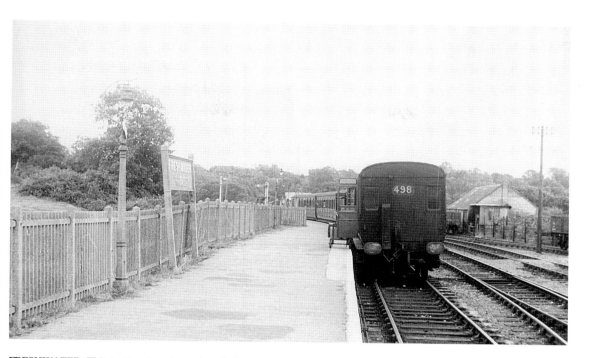

FRESHWATER: This is the view from the platform looking towards Yarmouth on 3 September 1952. The train is the 3.25pm to Newport.

In 2004 the site was occupied by several businesses, namely a supermarket at the buffer-stop end, then a garden centre and café, the latter named 'End of Line'. The raised land behind the supermarket forms a car park from which can be seen the present-day matching view. *H. C. Casserley/TG*

FRESHWATER: The two 'past' photographs of the station were taken on 3 June 1921 and 9 September 1952. Several alterations were made by the SR between 1927 and 1932, including extending the platform. In the upper photograph the locomotive, purchased second-hand by the FYNR in 1913, has recently arrived with its train of antiquated coaches as the 4.55pm service from Newport. It became No 1, and when the company was absorbed by the SR it was named *Medina* and used at Medina Wharf until 1932. The second photograph is again the 3.25pm to Newport.

Because of the buildings an exact match with the past is not possible, but this is as close as can be obtained. The building at the entrance to the goods yard shown in the 'past' photographs can be seen here. *H. C. Casserley/ R. M. Casserley/TG*

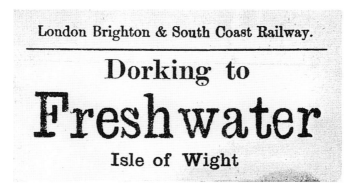

London Brighton & South Coast Railway.

Dorking to

Freshwater

Isle of Wight

Newport to Merstone

SHIDE was the first station south of Newport, on the outskirts of the town on the main road to Sandown. This view is looking towards Newport in the 1950s and shows No 33 *Bembridge* on a Sandown train. Note the ballast wagons just visible behind the last coach.

The station has been demolished and the road realigned, with a new main road to the east of the station. This is the view across what was the main road showing the building, on the right, occupying the station site in spring 2004. A cycle path uses the trackbed south from this point to Merstone. *IWSR Archive/TG*

A combined rail and bus ticket, Shide to Blackgang

BLACKWATER station, with its single platform, is seen here facing Sandown in early SR days. The girder bridge beneath the near (Newport) end of the platform spans the River Medina, here not much more than a brook. Immediately beyond the station building was a level crossing on the main road to Shanklin.

The station building still stands and the site is privately owned. An extension in the same style as the original building has been added on the platform side. The trackbed is not accessible to the public and the cycle path takes a minor diversion, returning to the trackbed beyond the main road. *IWSR Archive/TG*

Opposite MERSTONE: A two-coach push-pull set, consisting of ex-LBSCR vehicles newly painted in crimson livery, is berthed at Merstone in the spring of 1949. Note that 1st Class facilities were provided. This is one of the sets normally used for Ventnor West services.

Standing on the remains of the island platform on 9 April 2004, it is easy to picture the past scene in one's mind. The trackbed is being put to good use and over the course of about an hour the author saw plenty of cyclists. A small car park for cyclists and walkers is provided by the old platform. *Neil Sprinks/TG*

An SR ticket from Merstone to Horringford for 'One Musical Instrument, Typewriter or other article at Owner's Risk'!

Below This 19 August 1952 photograph shows the destination board of the through train referred to as 'The Tourist'. This name was not shown in the public timetable, but was displayed on the side of the coaches. *Neil Sprinks*

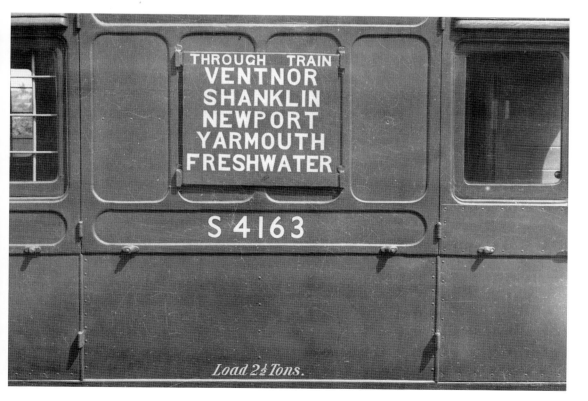

MERSTONE was a neat and attractive station, as seen on 27 June 1953. This view is looking towards Newport and a solitary wagon occupies the siding where the coaches shown on page 36 were berthed. Note the ladder used for lighting the oil lamp.

Today's view was taken during a pause between cyclists approaching from Shide. *H. C. Casserley/TG*

MERSTONE: On the right, the 4.25pm to Ventnor West, hauled by No 35 *Freshwater*, has the road. The train on the left is the 3.56pm from Cowes and will leave Merstone for Sandown and the other station at Ventnor behind No 27 *Merstone*. The station house is to the left across a minor road.

Bungalows now occupy the site of the station house. The line ran along the access road to more bungalows, with the junction of the Sandown and Ventnor West lines almost at the end of this road. *H. C. Casserley/TG*

MERSTONE: The 5.27pm train to Ventnor West has just left Merstone on 19 August 1952. The train comprises No 35 *Freshwater* and push-pull Set No 503, ex-LBSCR coaches Nos 4169 and 6367. These had been renumbered from 3828 and 6204 on transfer from the mainland by the SR. The station house can be seen beyond the rear coach.

Beyond the access road to the bungalows the Ventnor line trackbed is not used as a cycle path, but is on private land, seen here on 7 April 2004. The fence on the left marks the old railway boundary. *Neil Sprinks/TG*

Merstone to Ventnor West

GODSHILL station, which became a halt in 1928, was situated outside and to the west of the village on a descending approach road. Its proximity to a farm is apparent in this photograph taken on 3 September 1952 from a train bound for Ventnor West.

The farm was still very much in evidence during the 2004 visit. The station building is in use as a domestic dwelling and has had additional rooms built on the platform. *H. C. Casserley/TG*

WHITWELL HALT: Photographed on 9 November 1928, the passing loop at Whitwell is shortly to be taken out, and the station was demoted to halt status in 1941.

The main buildings have all been retained, the station house being available to let for holidays, and the trackbed has been filled in through the station to platform level. Overall this is a very attractive location, capturing the spirit of the long defunct railway. *H. C. Casserley/TG*

ST LAWRENCE HALT was another station in a cramped position at aptly named Undercliff, and became an unstaffed halt in 1927. As seen in the photographs the railway was crossed by a road on a sharp bend and steep hill, incorporating a 'tee' junction. The 'past' view is looking towards Ventnor West on 3 September 1952.

In 2004 the station site was in private hands, with the station house as the main dwelling and the course of the railway in use as a garden. *H. C. Casserley/TG*

VENTNOR WEST station was high above the town and inconveniently situated at the western extremity at a location known as Steephill. Despite its location, it was called Ventnor Town until being renamed by the SR in 1923. A single ex-LBSCR push-pull coach was often used on the line, as seen here in the spring of 1949. For many years the trains were worked by Class 'A1X' tanks, but here Class 'O2' No 36 *Carisbrooke*, recently arrived from the mainland, is being used.

The author's first visit to Ventnor West was on 28 December 1955, three years after closure. Apart from the removal of track, little had changed. The roofs of buildings in the background show how high the station was above the nearby road.

The former station approach road now continues through a housing estate. The most surprising feature is that the old station building has been retained and is a private house. The road from which the 'present' photograph was taken was constructed over the trackbed. *Neil Sprinks/TG (2)*

VENTNOR WEST: The 4.25pm train from Merstone hauled by No 35 *Freshwater* has arrived at Ventnor West on 3 September 1952, just two weeks prior to closure.

On 19 March 1960 the land surrounding the station was being cleared, with the expectation that the station building would be demolished. In fact, only a section nearest to the camera was taken down and the remainder converted into a splendid house for private occupation.

The present-day view clearly shows the foreshortened house, in attractive residential surroundings. *R. M. Casserley (2)/TG*

Merstone to Sandown

HORRINGFORD: The main road from Newport to Sandown was dissected at Horringford by the railway running between the same two towns. There was a single-platform station, seen here in SR days, with the crossing at the far (Sandown) end.

The station building and surrounding land are now privately owned. The cycle path leaves the course of the railway to the Merstone side of the station and rejoins it from the main road at the Sandown end. *IWSR Archive/TG*

NEWCHURCH was a smaller station, with a wooden building. On 28 December 1955 No 31 *Chale* approaches the station with the second train of the day. This was a miserable and disappointing day, as it was the author's only opportunity to travel on the line, which was due to close a few weeks later on 6 February.

Despite the lack of a railway, a visit in April 2004 was more enjoyable, with dry and warm weather. A bungalow occupies the site of the station, and as elsewhere the cycle path makes a minor diversion. Beyond the bungalow, as seen here, the public path takes up the course of the railway, although a few bends seem to have been introduced.

ALVERSTONE was a little more substantial and even had a siding. This view is looking towards Newport in SR days. Note the odd crossing gates, presumably either a routine renewal or the result of an accident.

The present-day location is easily identified by the former station house. There is no diversion of the cycle path round the station site. *IWSR Archive/TG*

ALVERSTONE: Looking in the other direction on 27 June 1953, we see the 1.08pm service from Sandown to Cowes approaching. The minor road in the foreground offers an alternative route between Ventnor and Brading, bypassing Shanklin and Sandown. Even today it is a tortuous and hence a slow route. The station building and surrounding land is in private use. *H. C. Casserley/TG*

Newport towards Smallbrook Junction

WHIPPINGHAM was the first station out of Newport on the Ryde line. It closed to passengers on 21 September 1953, but was still staffed when this photograph was taken on 29 December 1955. There was a crossing loop from 1912, and exchange of tokens took place here until 1956, when the up side was taken out.

The station building is now used as a private house, which can just be seen behind the trees separating the public path from the grounds of the house.

WOOTTON station consisted of a single platform on a curve, with no crossing loop, and closed on the same date as Whippingham. This view is looking toward Havenstreet (then spelled Haven Street) in the early 1950s. There are no buildings on the platform, as these are located under one of the bridge arches.

The station has been demolished and the bridge filled in. The public path terminates at the road, as immediately on the other side of the site of the bridge is a new Wootton station. *IWSR Archive/TG*

WOOTTON: The new station is seen under construction on 19 October 1978, looking toward Newport. It will be the western terminus of the Isle of Wight Steam Railway's line from Smallbrook Junction.

The station opened on 7 August 1986, and a visit on 5 May 2004 found a beautiful replica of a typical SR country station, complete with a concrete nameboard, LSWR-style lamp posts and even a grounded van body. *Barry Thirlwall/TG*

HAVENSTREET: This attractive view of Haven Street (as it was then known) was taken from the window of a train from Cowes on 12 August 1965. In the platform is a Ryde to Cowes train. Haven Street is virtually halfway between Ryde and Cowes, and the trains had left their respective points of origin within 6 minutes of each other. It has been the crossing point for trains since the station was rebuilt and a loop incorporated in 1926.

From being just a crossing point, Haven Street (now Havenstreet) has become the focal point of the Isle of Wight Steam Railway. The same view in 2004 finds that everything on the platform is still in order. In addition, there is a large building on the right, which is the railway's Works and engine shed.

HAVENSTREET: This photograph could easily have been taken in the 1950s, but in fact it is 14 August 1987, looking in the direction of Newport. The coach in the foreground was built by the SECR and became SR No 3402. On transfer to the Isle of Wight it was renumbered 4149; metal sheeting has replaced the original wooden panelling and the guard's 'birdcage' has been removed.

Another visit on 5 May 2004 found that new sidings were being laid in what was until recently a field, never before used for railway purposes. The approaching train, seen from the end of the platform, is from Wootton and is being hauled by Class 'A1X' No 8 *Freshwater*, the former FYNR engine. It was named *Freshwater* by the SR until it was returned to the mainland in 1949 to become No 32646.

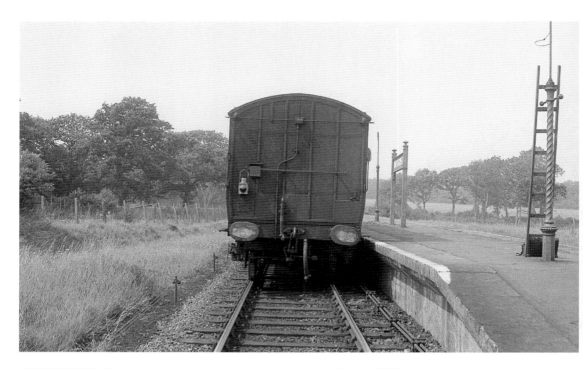

HAVENSTREET: The rather uninteresting view showing the back of an LBSCR coach at Havenstreet, also shows to the left a grassed embankment and the railway perimeter fence. This area has been transformed and the August 1987 view shows that the railway has expanded, with sidings and a large building (the Works) on the site. The diesel locomotive is named *Tiger*, built in 1953 and formerly at the Esso oil refinery at Fawley. Behind this is Class 'O2' No 24 *Calbourne*. In the station are various pre-Grouping vehicles and some SR utility vans. The covered van immediately beyond the coaches was originally a cattle wagon built by the LBSCR.

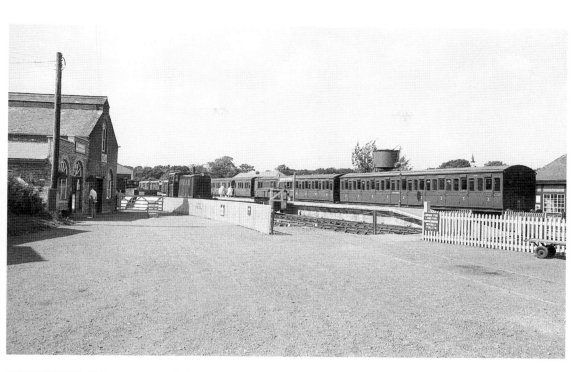

HAVENSTREET: This more general view of facilities at Havenstreet was also taken in August 1987 and shows the former gasworks building on the left, currently in use as a shop and museum for the railway. The water tower behind the train once stood at the Cowes end of Newport station. The locomotive coaling stage is just beyond the far end of the museum. The all-3rd Class coach on the right is No 2416; it was built by the LBSCR as a Brake 3rd (SR No 4019) and rebuilt on transfer to the Island. Improvements have been made to the site in the succeeding years, but it is still instantly recognisable as the same place.

SOUTHERN RAILWAY.
Issued subject to the Bye-laws, Regulations &
Conditions in the Company's Bills and Notices.

Ashey to
HAVEN STREET

THIRD CLASS
Fare 4½d.
NOT TRANSFERABLE

HAVENSTREET: The daily freight train from Medina Wharf passes through Haven Street on 12 August 1965 behind No 20 *Shanklin*. The signalman and driver have just exchanged tokens.

There was no freight train in evidence on 14 August 1987, but its place was occupied by a four-wheeled coach. This had arrived second-hand on the Island in 1897, bought by the IWR. It was withdrawn in 1926 and used as a holiday chalet on Hayling Island, returning to the Isle of Wight in 1975. In 1986 it was restored to near original condition, except for the underframe, which is from SR utility van No 1750, built in 1938. The coach carries No 6336, the number allocated to it by the SR.

HAVENSTREET: Departing for Ryde on 12 August 1965 is No 22 *Brading*. This event continues to be repeated to the present day, and on 5 May 2004 Class 'A1X' No 8 *Freshwater* leaves in the same direction with the 12.20 service from Wootton. It will, however, only run as far as Smallbrook Junction, where passengers for Ryde and the ferries to the mainland will change on to an electric train.

HAVENSTREET: The trains crossing at Haven Street in the summer of 1965 are, on the left, No 21 *Sandown* bound for Ryde, and on the right No 20 *Shanklin* on a Cowes train.

Sidings have been laid on the grassed area for the locomotive yard and shed. No 8 *Freshwater* is seen leaving the locomotive yard prior to working the 14.15 service to Smallbrook Junction. *Lawrence Golden/TG*

HAVENSTREET: The 'past' photograph shows diesel locomotive No D2554 three years after it was acquired by the IWSR. In 2004 its place in the siding had been taken by Class 'A1X' No 11 *Newport*, a name applied by the SR in 1930. It returned to the mainland in 1947 and later became BR No 32640. This former IWCR engine came back to the Island in 1973.

ASHEY consisted of a passing loop and two platforms until 1926, when the loop ceased to be used. The engine in this August 1965 view is No 24 *Calbourne*, which can still be seen here today.

On a visit in May 2004 the IWSR's 'A1X' No 8 *Freshwater* was in use rather than *Calbourne*, and is seen approaching the same point on the 14.15 service from Havenstreet to Smallbrook Junction.

ASHEY: No 24 *Calbourne* is seen again, this time working the 5.30pm Ryde Pier Head to Cowes service at the height of the summer holiday season in 1960. Note that in this photograph the train is using the former up platform and the down platform has been dismantled. The down platform was re-instated by BR in 1961 and the track realigned because of subsidence of the up platform. The station was operated as an unstaffed halt and closed on 20 February 1966.

On 5 May 2004 Class 'A1X' No 8 *Freshwater* returns from Smallbrook Junction on the 14.35 service to Wootton. The platform on the old down side was re-opened by the IWSR on 2 May 1993 and is still in use, trains stopping only by request. There is footpath but no public road access to the station.

ASHEY: The station house was in a derelict state at this 1965 visit and the old up platform had been demolished. The station house has since been renovated and is now in private ownership. The up line was behind the fence.

NEAR SMALLBROOK JUNCTION: The train is the 4.30pm from Ryde Pier Head to Cowes, photographed between Smallbrook Junction and Ashey on 22 August 1960. The engine is No 35 *Freshwater* and the train a mixture of LBSCR and SECR coaches constituting Set No 488 and a loose coach.

On 9 April 2004 No 198 *Royal Engineer* works the 11.53 Smallbrook Junction to Wootton service. This engine was built in 1953 and is on loan from the National Army Museum.

Ventnor to Brading

VENTNOR: The author's first visit to Ventnor was on 25 April 1957, when the locomotive (No 33 *Bembridge*) took temporary precedence over the young lady with the scarf on the right. The scarf has long since worn out, but the lady survives and travels with the aid of a Senior Railcard.

A visit was made alone on 9 April 2004, and although the station has gone, the area is still well used, now as an industrial estate.

VENTNOR: The 3.25pm from Ryde emerges from the tunnel under St Boniface Down and almost immediately enters Ventnor station. The engine is No 33 *Bembridge* again, this time on 14 May 1961.

The location is still accessible, except that the tunnel mouth has been blocked, the land in front being used by Southern Water.

VENTNOR: An excellent general view of the station was possible from St Boniface Down. On 14 May 1961 No 24 *Calbourne* is ready to leave with the 1.30pm train to Ryde Pier Head. The other engine is No 20 *Shanklin*, which has recently arrived on a Ramblers' Excursion from Ryde.

The same view today is partially blocked, but the main features of the site are still visible in May 2004.

WROXALL: The noon departure from Ventnor to Ryde Pier Head is seen a little south of Wroxall in July 1964 with No 35 *Freshwater* at the head. The line descends all the way from the north end of Ventnor Tunnel through Wroxall, Shanklin and Sandown, at a maximum of 1 in 70.

The same location is now overgrown and the downs in the background are partly obscured, even in the early spring of 2004.

WROXALL: This is the south end of the station, with No 21 *Sandown* pulling away with the 10.25am Ryde Pier Head to Ventnor train in July 1964. There was a loop here, installed in 1925 when a second platform was added for down trains. Wroxall and Ventnor were both closed on 18 April 1966, when the line south of Shanklin was abandoned.

The station site has been redeveloped for industrial use and the buildings of a timber company cover the old tracks through the station. Further industrial premises occupy the trackbed beyond the road overbridge at the north end of the station. The roof of one of the buildings on the embankment shown in the 'past' photograph is just visible.

SHANKLIN: This is the country end of the station in July 1964, with the 2.05pm service from Ryde Pier Head to Ventnor being hauled by No 22 *Brading*. Immediately behind the camera is a bridge under which passes a minor road. Shanklin was a substantial station with a passing loop and goods yard, and was well used by both local people and holidaymakers.

Shanklin became the southern terminus of the line on electrification. It was not only the station that was modified, but also the road. The bridge has been removed, the road upgraded and an access road to a new park resort added.

SHANKLIN: A few days before the end of steam in the winter of 1966, No 27 *Merstone* enters Shanklin on a train for Ryde. The third rail has already been laid in preparation for the new trains the following year.

Both platforms continued to be used following electrification, but a visit in August 1987 found that the old up platform was out of use and the track removed. This is the view looking towards Ventnor on 6 May 2004.

SHANKLIN: A special train for Ventnor approaches Shanklin in May 1961 hauled by No 20 *Shanklin*. On summe
Saturdays some trains ran only as far as here, hence the train in the siding on the right.

The sidings have all been taken out, but at least there is still a frequent passenger service. Here Class 483 N
007 arrives as the 08.23 service from Ryde Pier Head. There is only a 6-minute layover, after which the trai
returns to Ryde, in this instance full to standing. This unit is painted in London Transport red with gold letterin;
The set number, which on other units is displayed on the left-hand front of the driver's cab, is in the centre an
in the style of a Underground duty number.

LAKE: The present station at Lake was opened in July 1987, long after the cessation of steam workings. There was originally a halt here, which closed around the beginning of the First World War. Just one month after opening, Class 485 No 485043 enters Lake on a train to Ryde.

The station has grown in popularity and the author found on a visit in May 2004 that whatever the time of day there were always passengers using it. The more modern stock of Class 483, in this case No 007, approaches Lake on an evening train to Ryde Pier Head.

SANDOWN: With Sandown station in the background, No 29 *Alverstone* pounds up the bank towards Shanklin with the 4.05pm train from Ryde Pier Head to Ventnor in July 1964.

The same vantage point is no longer accessible as houses have been built adjacent to the lineside. However, there is a public boarded crossing a little further from the station, which gives a very similar viewpoint. On 5 May 2004 Class 483 No 006 forms the 18.17 service from Shanklin to Ryde Pier Head.

SANDOWN consisted of a down platform, on which the main building was situated, while on the up side was an island platform, in the centre of which was a high-level signal box. The outer face of the island was normally used by trains to Newport until closure of that line in 1956. This is the view of that far platform, looking towards Ryde on 5 October 1975. The signal box can be seen protruding through the platform canopy. The locomotive is diesel-mechanical Class 05 No 05001, built in 1956, in use on an engineers' train. It arrived on the Island in the autumn of 1966 as D2554 and was sold to the IWSR in 1984 (see page 64).

The loop was still in place on this visit in 1987, but by this time the canopy had been removed from the platform, making the signal box look rather more impressive. The grounded body in the foreground is one of the Underground motor coaches built in 1931-34, numbered 083569 in the Internal User series. It was formerly S19S of unit 043.

There has since been further change at Sandown, and the third view, looking in the same direction, taken in the spring of 2004, finds that some clearance has taken place in preparation for building works. *Barry Thirlwall/TG (2)*

SANDOWN: On 25 April 1957 Class 'E1' No 3 *Ryde* waits in the loop with a freight train for Ryde St John's Road
This platform was also used on summer Saturdays for trains to Ryde that started from Sandown.

All that remains on the up platform is a modern 'bus shelter'. There is no longer any track serving the fa
platform face, although there is still a siding along this side of the railway.

SANDOWN is seen from the Ryde end of the station in better times. Leaving for Ryde is No 24 *Calbourne* on the 1.40pm train from Ventnor on 4 August 1959.

On 14 August 1987 trains cross at the station: on the left is Class 486 No 486031, and on the right is the next consecutively numbered unit. The now redundant lattice-post gantry signal has gone, its place being taken by an SR-style rail-built starter. The parcels bay on the left has been filled in, but there are still sidings on the far right.

SANDOWN: Following closure, the remnant of the line to Newport was used for storing goods stock. There were also sidings here, and redundant wagons were dumped in the weeks prior to the temporary closure of the Sandown to Ryde line in the winter of 1966.

This area was later used by the engineers' department for berthing its vehicles, including Class 03 diesel shunter No 03079, formerly D2079, seen in the second photograph on 14 August 1987.

By 2004 the track had been removed and part of the land sold for residential development, but there is still a siding close to the running road.

3rd-SINGLE   SINGLE-3rd

0517

Ryde Pier Head to

Ryde Pier Head   Ryde Pier Head
Sandown   Sandown

SANDOWN

(S)   1/2 FARE 1/2   (S)

For conditions see over For conditions see over

0517

SANDOWN: The 2.25pm from Ryde Pier Head to Ventnor is worked by No 14 *Fishbourne*, and is seen approaching Sandown on 4 August 1959. Note the activity in the coal yard on the right.

Prior to laying the third rail, clearance tests on the recently acquired Underground stock were made, and here No 24 *Calbourne* is seen with an ex-LBSCR box van as match truck and a solitary Underground coach numbered 037. This was to be the number of a spare 3-VEC unit, but the plan was abandoned. By this time the coal yard had closed.

In May 2004 more modern Underground stock in the form of Class 483 No 006 passes the same point. There is not even a trace of the coal yard, as houses have been built right up to the running lines. *TG/Lawrence Golden/TG*

BRADING: Between Sandown and Brading the line had been doubled in 1927, and at Yarbridge, about half a mile south of Brading, the railway passes under a road bridge from which there are good views of the railway in both directions. A down train in the last summer of steam operations is hauled by No 35 *Freshwater*. Brading station is in the background.

The line was singled in 1988, and seen from the same bridge in May 2004 is Class 483 No 007 bound for Shanklin. The station is hidden from view by trees, but the house high in the left background can still be seen. *Lawrence Golden/TG*

BRADING: There is a public footpath alongside the railway from Yarbridge to Brading, which in steam days was not fenced. On 4 August 1959 No 14 *Fishbourne* heads towards Ryde on the 12.40pm train from Ventnor. Outside the peak season, coaches were stored in a siding adjacent to this stretch of line.

Although there is now a fence, this does not interrupt the view of the railway. The footpath was rather overgrown when the author arrived here on 6 May 2004, but by the time he left several hours later it had been cleared by local authority contractors. This is the rear of No 006 forming the 09.23 service from Ryde Pier Head to Shanklin.

BRADING: The noon train from Ventnor enters the station on 22 August 1960. The coaches constitute Set No 492 which is being hauled by No 18 *Ningwood*. The nearer of the two boarded crossings is the railway barrow crossing; the second a public footpath; the latter is still open, while the former has been removed because the down island platform has been abandoned. The storage siding can just be seen behind the last coach.

The line was still double in 1987, but the siding had been removed. Unit No 486031 is about to cross the public footpath as it approaches the station.

BRADING: On the extreme right of this general view of the station, looking north in the summer of 1966, the abandoned platform for Bembridge can be seen. No 17 *Seaview* enters the station on a train for Shanklin.

Class 485 No 485044 has just arrived on a Ryde Pier Head train on 14 August 1987. The Bembridge side of the station has become overgrown, with the signal box now isolated from the railway. Both main lines were in use at the time of this visit, but now the up platform is used for trains in both directions. The footbridge has been closed to the public and there is no access to the island platform.

BRADING: On 22 August 1960 the 12.05pm train from Ryde Pier Head consists of No 14 *Fishbourne* and Set N 500, and is waiting to leave Brading for Ventnor. The signal box can be seen to the right of the island platform.

The second photograph, taken on 26 May 2004, shows how far nature has spread towards the island platform. The signal box is still in place, although becoming increasingly dilapidated. Class 483 No 002 forms the 16.1 service from Shanklin to Ryde Pier Head.

BRADING: Seen from the point where the Bembridge line used to diverge is the noon Ventnor to Ryde train hauled by No 31 *Chale* on 4 August 1959. The small goods yard is still open and contains a couple of box vans of LBSCR origin.

This location still affords a good view of the station, despite the encroaching bushes and trees. The train is the 09.53 service from Shanklin, formed of Class 483 No 006 on 6 May 2004.

BRADING: Representing a typical summer train on the Isle of Wight, with a well turned-out engine and long train, the engine is, appropriately, No 22 *Brading* with the 5.25pm service from Ryde Pier Head to Ventnor, seen a short distance north of Brading. It is July 1964 and it seems unreal that trains like this would no longer be running within 2½ years. In the foreground is a boarded crossing that forms part of a footpath from Brading toward St Helens. The Bembridge branch ran close to the line of low trees in the right background.

The crossing is still open, and on 26 May 2004 a prehistoric beast is wrapping its claws round a somewhat younger Class 483 No 002, which is named *Raptor*, forming the 16.08 service from Ryde Pier Head.

Brading to Bembridge

T HELENS: The author's first visit to St Helens on the Bembridge branch was on 21 September 1955, two years fter closure. Everything was still intact, and although weeds were growing on the trackbed, some present-day pen stations on the national network are in a worse state than this! There was a quay at St Helens with rail ccess, which was very busy until superseded by the rebuilt Medina Wharf in 1928.

The station and surrounding area is all now private property. The same view today shows a beautifully restored ation building, with some modifications and additions that blend in well with the original building.

ST HELENS: A short distance beyond the station the railway crossed an inlet. On 4 April 1953 the 3.28pm from Bembridge to Brading is worked by No 14 *Fishbourne* and two-coach Set No 505.

There have been significant changes here, with sluice gates and a pumping station, but the location is still recognisable. The bridge in the background carries the road to Bembridge, which runs in front of the block of flats. *Neil Sprinks/TG*

BEMBRIDGE station is seen on the same day, showing the neatly kept terminus with adjacent small goods yard. This is the view looking toward the buffer-stops.

The old-fashioned charm of this location has been ruined by recent housing development, which has managed to almost totally eliminate everything connected with the railway. *Neil Sprinks/TG*

Opposite BEMBRIDGE: This pleasant end-of-the-line shot, taken on 3 September 1952, shows No 14 *Fishbourne* about to run round its train before making another trip to Brading.

In the uninspiring present-day view, the main road, which has run parallel to the railway from St Helens and is immediately beyond the trees, almost wraps itself round the site of the station by turning sharply south as it climbs the hill into Bembridge itself. *H. C. Casserley/TG*

Below The destination board displayed on the side of one of the branch coaches in April 1953. *Neil Sprinks*

Brading towards Smallbrook Junction

NORTH OF BRADING: The 12.05pm train from *Ryde Pier Head* to *Ventnor* is hauled by No 36 *Carisbrooke* on 4 August 1959. At this point the line is descending, the summit being about a mile back. There has only ever been single track between Brading and Smallbrook Junction.
On 5 May 2004 Class 483 No 007 passes the same point forming the 10.23 Ryde Pier Head to Shanklin service. This is the first down train of the day to stop at Smallbrook Junction, which is only served when trains are running on the IWSR.

NORTH OF BRADING: This is another pleasant location between Brading and Smallbrook Junction. On 22 August 1960 the 1.00pm train from Ventnor consists of Set No 500 being hauled by No 14 *Fishbourne*.

The same stretch of line on 4 May 2004 sees Class 483 No 006 forming the 10.13 service from Shanklin, the first up train of the day to stop at Smallbrook Junction.

Smallbrook Junction to Ryde Pier Head

SMALLBROOK JUNCTION signal box was only open during summer months – it had no road access and there was no station. Opened in 1926, it closed 40 years later, and this is the view from the window of the 6.20pm train from Ventnor to Ryde passing the box in July 1964. The train is about to leave the single-line section.

Smallbrook Junction station was opened on 20 July 1991 exclusively as an interchange point between the Ryde to Shanklin trains and the steam trains to Havenstreet and Wootton. There is still no road, nor even a public footpath to Smallbrook Junction. There is, however, an access path for railway staff. On 6 May 2004 Class 483 No 006 makes an unscheduled stop to pick up the author long after the last train had left for Havenstreet.

SMALLBROOK JUNCTION is seen here looking towards Ventnor (the line on the left) and Newport (right) in 1960 when both lines were open. The train is the 3.00pm from Ventnor to Ryde Pier Head, with No 26 *Whitwell* hauling Set No 491.

On 6 May 2004 Class 483 No 006 is just pulling away from the Shanklin platform, which serves both up and down trains between Ryde and Shanklin. The platform for Havenstreet is at a slightly higher level.

SMALLBROOK JUNCTION: The 3.30pm train from Ryde to Cowes has just negotiated the junction and is heading for Ashey on 22 August 1960 formed of No 24 *Calbourne* and Set No 486. The signal box can be seen in the background.

The present-day view of the approach to Smallbrook Junction clearly shows the new station. *Calbourne* still frequents this location on trains to and from Wootton, but on 5 May 2004 Class A1X No 8 *Freshwater* was being used.

SMALLBROOK JUNCTION: On 22 August 1960 No 17 *Seaview* works the 3.05pm Ryde Pier Head to Ventnor train with Sets Nos 488 and 497. It is about to leave the double-track section at the junction.

On 5 May 2004 Class 483 No 007 approaches the single-line section immediately before the interchange platform. On the left is the end of the line from Havenstreet.

SOUTH OF RYDE: The line descends from Smallbrook Junction all the way to Ryde St John's Road, and passes through some attractive wooded scenery before reaching the outskirts of the seaside town. Here No 36 *Carisbrooke* takes the 5.20pm from Ventnor towards Ryde, while in the comparative view, dated 6 May 2004, Class 483 No 002 forms an afternoon train to Shanklin.

SOUTH OF RYDE: The 5.30pm train from Ryde Pier Head to Cowes is seen climbing between St John's Road and Smallbrook Junction on 4 August 1959 behind No 17 *Seaview*. The double-track as far as Smallbrook was only used in conventional up and down mode in the summer. For the remainder of the year, when the box was switched out, the line on the left was used only by trains to and from Newport, and on the right by Ventnor trains.

The same location is less accessible in 2004 and Class 483 No 006 is seen almost emerging from the undergrowth, in keeping with its 'dinosaur' image.

RYDE ST JOHN'S ROAD: The steep climb out of St John's Road to Smallbrook Junction is tackled on 4 August 1959 by No 31 *Chale*, with the 5.25pm from Ryde Pier Head to Ventnor. The first two coaches are ex-LBSCR and the others SECR. The town forms an attractive backdrop.

Much of the town is hidden by trees in this August 1987 view. Class 485 No 485045 tackles the bank with the 5.10 service from Pier Head to Shanklin.

RYDE ST JOHN'S ROAD: The trains crossing outside St John's Road station on 22 August 1960 are, on the left, N 31 *Chale* on the 6.05pm from Pier Head to Ventnor, with the first coach of Set No 490, while in the centre is N 26 *Whitwell* with the 5.40pm from Ventnor. The coaches on the right are berthed.

The sidings on the right have been taken out, but both up and down running roads are still very much in us This is Class 485 No 485043 heading for Shanklin as the 16.30 service from Pier Head.

YDE ST JOHN'S ROAD: Pulling away from the station on 22 August 1960 is No 14 *Fishbourne* and Set No 492
~~rming~~ the 6.25pm train to Ventnor. The engine shed is to the left of the signal box and the Works to the right
~~f~~ the train. The signal box is of SECR origin and came from Waterloo East in 1928.
  A visit on 4 August 1987 found that the shed and yard had gone and most of the land was out of use. The signal
~~ox~~ is, however, still operational and the down starter is off for Class 485 No 485043, on its way to Shanklin.

RYDE ST JOHN'S ROAD: No 14 *Fishbourne* drifts into the station in the summer of 1960 with an evening train t[o] Ventnor consisting of Set No 492. A few wagons can be seen outside the Works.

The station, signal box and Works are all still operational. The obvious change is the new footbridge connectin[g] the up and down platforms; a footbridge used to be located at the other end of the station by the road overbridg[e.] Class 483 No 007 has just arrived forming a late afternoon train from Shanklin.

New, or rather second-hand, stock arrives on the Island in the form of an Underground coach in November 1966. It is already painted in British Railways' Rail Blue livery and carries set number 042. The entrance to the yard is a short distance down the hill behind the camera on the left-hand side just prior to the station entrance.

RYDE ST JOHN'S ROAD: Another coach being delivered by road to the yard on the same day. It will form part of Set No 046, and has been railed via the ramp in the background.

On 18 October 1973 the yard was in use by the engineer's department; the diesel shunter is D2554.

Since then the track has been removed, as seen in the 2004 photograph. Part of the yard is in use by a builders' merchants and is separated from the running roads by a fence. *TG/Barry Thirlwall/TG*

RYDE SHED was built on this site in 1930. No 36 *Carisbrooke* is seen at the shed on 29 December 1955. The previous day it had run into a tree that had fallen across the line at Brading; only superficial damage was suffered, although the line was closed for several hours. No 36 was withdrawn in June 1964. The entrance road to the yard is out of sight on the left.

This is the site of the shed in 2004, oddly enough with two Underground coach bodies in the undergrowth. These are surplus coaches of the erstwhile set No 483010.

RYDE SHED: Nos 30 *Shorwell* and 27 *Merstone* stand outside St John's Road shed on 22 August 1960. No 30 was withdrawn in September 1965, but No 27 survived until the end of 1966. Twelve of the 'O2s' were allocated here in the 1950s, the remainder at Newport. The same location in 1987 looks rather run-down, with the track removed and an odd collection of huts in its place, and it is little different in 2004.

RYDE SHED: Of the four Class 'E1s' on the Island, one (No 4) was allocated to Ryde and the remainder to Newport until closure of the latter in November 1957. This is No 3 *Ryde*, dumped alongside the engine shed on 4 August 1959, having been condemned three months earlier. A coal depot occupied part of the shed site in 1987, but even this is no more today.

RYDE ST JOHN'S ROAD: No 18 *Ningwood* undertakes some shunting on the down main line in the final weeks of regular steam operation in the winter of 1966. This location is immediately north of St John's Road station, looking towards Esplanade.

The line on the extreme right was used to dump withdrawn Class 483 No 001 in 2004. Attempts to minimise vandalism have been made by boarding up the windows. The line was the former down loop, now a siding.

RYDE ST JOHN'S ROAD WORKS: Unlike its sister engine, Class 'E1' No 4 *Wroxall* is undergoing repair and is seen outside the Works on the same day. This was the last survivor and was not condemned until October 1960.

The Works is still open, and is also used for berthing stock. Outside the works in 1987 are Class 485 Nos 485041 and 485044. The Works was rebuilt in 1938 and the more modern part, for carriage and wagon repairs, is to the left. It was upgraded again about a year after this photograph was taken, when the number of roads into the newer building was reduced from three to two.

The third photograph gives a more general recent view of the Works. Two of the 'dinosaur' units of Class 483 Nos 002 and 004, stand outside in May 2004.

RYDE ESPLANADE station was rather hemmed in, thereby restricting photography from the platforms. On this occasion, in the weeks prior to temporary closure of the whole system, the section from Esplanade to Pier Head had already closed for engineering works and trains were starting from Esplanade. This train, leaving from the up platform and headed by No 22, is waiting to depart for Shanklin. There is another engine on the rear, which will be taken off at St John's Road.

Removal of the canopy of the down platform, currently out of use, has enabled a better view of the station to be obtained. On 5 May 2004 Class 483 No 006 heads for Shanklin with a late afternoon service.

YDE ESPLANADE station is also visible from the Pier. To the left of the station on 14 August 1987, a hovercraft as recently arrived from Portsmouth. The train consists of Class 485 No 485045, about to undertake the final uarter-mile of its journey as the 16.00 service from Shanklin. The remains of the Pier tramway and its station are the right – the last tram ran in January 1969.

Little has changed in the 2004 view. There is still a hovercraft in sight, the tramway has become slightly more ecrepit, but the train is more modern, being Class 483 No 002.

RYDE PIER HEAD: With just three months to go before the end of steam, No 20 *Shanklin* pulls out of Pier Head for Ventnor. Today the signal box has gone, the site being adjacent to the rear coach of Class 483 No 002, seen on 5 May 2004.

RYDE PIER HEAD: On 22 August 1960 No 18 *Ningwood* approaches the terminus with Set No 497, forming the 4.40pm train from Ventnor. One of the Pier trams is just beyond the signal box, while on the extreme right is the Pier access road.

The replacement electric trains are represented by Class 485 No 485045 in the summer of 1987.

RYDE PIER HEAD: A closer view of Pier Head station in the summer of 1960 shows two island platforms. In the centre is No 17 *Seaview* on the 7.35pm Cowes train. On the extreme right is No 24 *Calbourne*, which will work the 7.25pm to Ventnor.

Twenty-seven years later two Class 485 units (485045 and 485041) are seen at Pier Head. Note that the platform canopy on the right has been shortened and there is no longer rail access to the far face of this platform, as this was removed in 1966. The other platform has been widened, so that the remaining line between the islands is served by both platforms; passengers board trains on the west side and leave on the east side.

Further reduction in facilities had taken place by 2004. Despite the present-day frequent service, in between trains Pier Head looks like an abandoned station. Only the far left platform is in regular use, as the line from the south end of Esplanade station has been singled. On the positive side, the trains make excellent connections with the frequent ferries to Portsmouth Harbour, and waiting rooms are provided at both Esplanade and Pier Head.

BRITISH TRANSPORT COMMISSION (S)
RYDE PIER
ADMIT
ONE
PERSON 3D
FOR CONDITIONS SEE OVER
4401375

INDEX OF LOCATIONS

London and South Western Ry.
787
From WATERLOO
TO
WHIPPINGHAM
Via **PORTSMOUTH.**

London and South Western Ry.
787
From WATERLOO TO
Whippingham
Via **STOKES BAY.**